WAYS OF THE SPIRIT

The Spirituality of Cardinal Suenens

WAYS OF THE SPIRIT

THE SPIRITUALITY OF
Cardinal Suenens

*Drawn from the writings of Cardinal Suenens
and edited with an introduction by
Elizabeth Hamilton*

A CROSSROAD BOOK
THE SEABURY PRESS • NEW YORK

1976
The Seabury Press
815 Second Avenue
New York, N.Y. 10017

The translations and editorial matter © 1976 Darton,
Longman and Todd Ltd. All the original texts from
which the translations have been made are the
copyright of Cardinal Suenens and are used with his
permission.

Grateful acknowledgment is extended to Paulist/
Newman Press for permission to use material from
Christian Life Day by Day, The Gospel to Every Creature, and
The Nun in the World.

Library of Congress Catalog Card Number: 76–46307
ISBN: 0–8164–1218–9
Printed in United States of America

CONTENTS

FOREWORD

I welcome this book of extracts from the writings of my dear friend, Cardinal Suenens.

The best way to profit from the book would be to read it slowly, over a long period, one brief section each day; to meditate on the words; and to make them the centre of one's prayer for that day.

It is my hope that, used in this way, these quotations will prove to be a means of spiritual enrichment to a wide variety of readers throughout the world. God speed them on their way and write them on our hearts.

DONALD CANTUAR

EDITOR'S NOTE

I want to thank Cardinal Suenens for having approved the publication of this book.

His generosity in giving help and encouragement, as well as reading the final typescript in its entirety, is characteristic of the Cardinal's readiness, despite the many demands on his time, to put himself at the disposal of others.

The majority of the excerpts I translated myself from the original french. A few, however have been taken from writings and addresses that were composed in english originally.

ELIZABETH HAMILTON

WAYS OF THE SPIRIT

The Spirituality of Cardinal Suenens

INTRODUCTION

God is love.
God loves each one of us with the totality of his
    love.
God knows us by name: 'I know my sheep and
    they know me.'
God keeps us in all our ways . . .

(Bristol 1973)

The voice which spoke these words was low-
pitched, conversational, friendly.

Cardinal Suenens is a good speaker: intelligent,
straightforward, uncomplicated, humorous. No
need for rhetorical devices. The quiet words of
themselves command attention. So do the eyes
that at a distance look darker than they are. If the
face in repose is at first sight somewhat sombre,
this is not for long. Soon it will light up with a
smile, as if illumined from within.

The poet William Blake, when asked if at dawn
he did not see a disc of fire – something like a
guinea, replied: 'Oh no, no, I see an innumerable

company of the heavenly host crying "Holy, Holy, Holy, is the Lord God Almighty." '

The thought behind the Cardinal's quiet words has, I believe, this quality. It is one with that of Antoine de Saint-Exupéry (a writer whom the Cardinal admires) in *Le Petit Prince: Ce qui est important ne se voit pas; l'essentiel est invisible pour les yeux.*

Cardinal Suenens is a man like ourselves, but wiser than we are – because more perceptive, more courageous, more joyous, more confident in the power of the Holy Spirit, one who by the grace of that same Spirit commends to us the Gospel message, in all gentleness, all courtesy.

Enthroned as Archbishop of Malines-Brussels in December 1961 and made a Cardinal by Pope John XXIII the following March, Léon-Joseph Suenens was an outstanding figure in the Second Vatican Council.

Working closely with the Pope both in the period preparatory to the Council and throughout the first session, he developed in outline, at the Holy Father's request, the form the conciliar deliberations should take. In brief, the Church was to be viewed in the light of a two-fold perspective: first, within, *ad intra* – in relation, that is, to its members collectively and individually; secondly, without, *ad extra,* in relation to all christians, indeed all human beings regardless of their religious beliefs.

14

Subsequently, chosen by Pope Paul as one of the four Moderators, he made an outstanding contribution towards the formulation of two major documents: the *Dogmatic Constitution on the Church*, or *Lumen Gentium*, and the *Constitution on the Church in the Modern World* or *Gaudium et Spes*.

Overcoming an innate shyness, as well as a disinclination to be involved in disputes or give offence to others, he spoke out fearlessly – resolutely determined that the Council should take all possible measures to bring about in the Church the *aggiornamento* of which Pope John had dreamed. One of his most important interventions concerned the charismatic dimension of the Church. Replying to Cardinal Ruffini who wanted to relegate charisms – gifts freely bestowed by the Holy Spirit – to the remote past, he stressed that the Church's charismatic dimension was essential to it today no less than formerly. What, he asked, would become of the Church without the charisms of doctors, theologians, prophets, men in every walk of life – and women also who, in virtue of the contribution they made to the Church, ought, he suggested, to be invited to attend the Council as auditors?

In the period that followed the Council the Cardinal continued to speak out, in interviews given to the press and in the Synods of Bishops convened at Rome. 'I know I shall be attacked,' he said, 'but I love the Church and the Pope, and I am ready to pay the price.'

The price was hostility, misunderstanding, misrepresentation – worst of all, the charge made against him, despite his repeated affirmations to the contrary, that he was disloyal to Pope Paul.

But since then, much water has flowed under the bridge.

In a general audience held in October 1974 Pope Paul warmly commended the Cardinal's newly published book about the Holy Spirit. 'I want to draw attention', he said, 'to a recent book written by Cardinal Suenens entitled *A New Pentecost?*'* In it he describes, and gives reasons for accepting as valid, what is known as charismatic renewal. The torrent of supernatural graces, or charisms, shows beyond any shadow of doubt that at this moment in the history of the Church, Providence is indeed at work.'

Then, in June 1975, at the close of the Charismatic Congress held in Rome, the Pope went a step further, when, not in his own name nor in that of the Church, but in the name of Christ, he thanked Cardinal Suenens in St Peter's basilica for what he had done and was doing to further charismatic renewal.

The Cardinal is indeed the one figure of real stature who can explain this phenomenon in terms of our own lives; he has a perceptivity, an

* London and New York 1975.

empathy, rare in ecclesiastics, which enables him to understand what is acceptable and helpful to the 'run-of-the mill' christian.

The support given to charismatic renewal by the Cardinal must be seen in relation to a life dedicated to the service of the Holy Spirit.

When on being made Auxiliary Bishop of Malines in 1955 he chose for his episcopal motto the words *In Spiritu Sancto,* this was more than a felicitous phrase: these were for him 'words of life'. Moreover an incident (it occurred during the Nazi occupation of Belgium) that prompted his choice, deserves mention. Summoned one day, in his capacity of Vice-Rector of Louvain, to the office of the Kreis-Kommandant, Graf von Thadden, grandson of Bismarck, he was so long in returning that it was feared he had been arrested. This was not so. The Commandant, having spoken briefly about some grievances the German authorities had against the University, went on to talk for a full hour of the overriding need for Christians to be united. A Protestant, interested in ecumenism, totally out of sympathy with Hitler, he said: 'What matters is that we experience together the communion of the Holy Spirit.'

'My motto *In Spiritu Sancto*', the Cardinal says, 'was an outcome of this encounter.'

The Holy Spirit, however, had not suddenly come down upon Suenens. Already in boyhood

17

his thoughts and aspirations were christocentric. Christ was all in all. He had the opportunity when approaching manhood of forging a career in the world of business where there was scope for his exceptional intelligence and enterprise. He refused. Christ was speaking to him. And Christ speaks through the voice of the Holy Spirit.

During the Council and the Synods, the Cardinal had been largely preoccupied with structural and governmental reforms which he saw not as an end in themselves, but as a means to an end – necessary if the Faithful were to be able to live the Gospel in its fulness. His real concern, however, is with persons. His spirituality, while founded on revealed truths that can be apprehended intellectually, is orientated towards 'experiencing' God as a person. He likes to recall Claudel's cry on the evening of his conversion: 'Lord, all of a sudden you have become a PERSON!' He writes in *A New Pentecost?* of times when 'God pierces the obscurity of faith like a flash of lightning in the darkness of the night'. He goes on: 'We may not be able to put these experiences into words. Indeed they are almost impossible to communicate; yet they are real, and lives are transformed by them'.

It is natural, then, that the Cardinal should be in sympathy with charismatics whose form of worship encourages spontaneity and a freedom of expression that can have an almost child-like quality.

18

This sympathy is apparent when the Cardinal takes part in a charismatic gathering: a prayer meeting or a mass. There is a rapport between himself and the participants; he is relaxed; he is happy to be praying with them, reaching out his arms with them. He appreciates, above all, their spirit of joy.

Addressing a gathering of some 25,000 charismatics at Notre Dame University, Indiana, he said to them:

'I love you because you praise God not for any ulterior motive, but for his own sake, for his glory ... By the power of the Holy Spirit you have discovered what adoration means.

'I love you because you are faithful both to the Father and to the Son. ...

'Be filled with the Holy Spirit and you will renew the face of the earth.'

Using as his yardstick the words of the Gospel: 'By their fruits you will know them', he has discovered from first-hand experience that, contrary to what is sometimes supposed, charismatic renewal fosters loyalty to the Church; recourse to the sacraments; love of the scriptures; concern for others both at a local and at a world level; respect and affection for the clergy – when the priests, vested for Mass, processed across the stadium at Notre Dame they were greeted with a thunder of applause.

The fact that the Cardinal has associated

himself with charismatic renewal has done much to make this same renewal acceptable, indeed 'respectable', among persons who, not wholly without reason, viewed it with suspicion. His presence lends a quiet dignity to a gathering which, if mishandled or left to its own devices, could all too easily give way to emotional excesses. Simply by being there, he exercises an authority that is totally unobtrusive. 'Because he does not try to dominate us', a young man said in Dublin, 'we are "open" to him – glad when he gives us a lead.'

Furthermore, by word of mouth and in his writings, the Cardinal, as a theologian, is able to explain in terms consonant with the teaching of the Church, aspects of charismatic renewal that to many persons present a problem: 'speaking in tongues', for example, and (more important) 'baptism in the Spirit'.

'The disciples were filled with joy and the Holy Spirit.' The charismatic experience is one of joy. The message that the Cardinal proclaims in season and out – yet not obtrusively – is one of joy. I write now of his message to all men. For it would be wrong to give the impression that his attention is focused solely on charismatic groups. His vision is too wide for that. What he says, he says to all: to regular members of charismatic prayer groups, certainly – but no less to those who 'drop in' from time to time; to those, too, who for one reason or another, do not attend these gatherings. Charismatics, he says, are not an élite.

Nor, in his view, does this form of renewal constitute a 'movement' with affiliated members, specific duties, and leaders holding positions of authority. It is, rather a 'current' of grace sent to remind us what we are by virtue of our baptism: one which, when its purpose is served, will disappear. He compares it to a river which, having reached its mouth and merged into the sea is, to all intents and purposes, no longer a river.

Charismatics are, he affirms, 'normal' christians. Equally, one might say that 'normal' christians − christians, that is, who are impregnated with the spirit of Christ, who live through and with and in Christ − are, in fact, charismatics, though they may not think of themselves in this way.

Mary, the Cardinal says, was the first charismatic, the first christian. Mary, through the action and the indwelling of the Holy Spirit, lived through and with and in her Son who was, likewise, the Son of God, her Creator and Redeemer.

And if we live united with Christ, *through Him, with Him and in Him . . . in the unity of the Holy Spirit,* what does this mean in terms of our daily lives? It means joy, hope, courage. It does not mean the elimination of suffering − Jesus suffered, and the

21

servant is not greater than his Master. It *does* mean that suffering is shot through with joy – more than that, outweighed by joy: a joy which, the Lord has told us, no man can take from us.

And if we rejoice, we must needs hope; for we rejoice because, St Paul says, we know in whom we hope. Hope, in the Cardinal's words, is a 'component factor of our very being'. And again he says: 'Hope derives from God, relys on God – on God alone'. He confesses himself a 'man of hope' – not for human reasons nor from a natural optimism, but because he believes in the Holy Spirit working within the world, within the Church, within the heart of each one of us. If we have joy and hope, then we have courage. Joy and hope leave no place for fear. They embolden us, fill our hearts with courage. 'Fear not, little flock.' And again: 'Be not troubled neither be afraid.'

Charismatic renewal makes an important contribution, the Cardinal believes, in the sphere of ecumenism, in that it encourages christians of differing allegiance to pray together. If Roman Catholics, for example, and members of the Orthodox and the Anglican Churches are praying together, they are already, to that extent, united, in that they are orientated towards Christ, asking for the guidance of Christ, waiting upon the will of Christ; looking together at Christ – united in a bond of love: love of God and love of one another. The Cardinal recalls in his writings and addresses a saying of Antoine de Saint-Exupéry that those who love each other look not so much at each other as ahead, in the same direction.

This 'looking at' Christ together is not intended as a substitute for theological discussion. The latter is essential if doctrinal differences are to be resolved. In the matter of visible union the Cardinal is a realist: he is content, if need be, merely to glimpse the Promised Land from afar, as did Moses when he stood on the heights of Nebo. He is content, yet not wholly satisfied. The delay in attaining this unity is, he believes largely our own making. We attribute to God 'patience' of a kind that is not his, but ours – lethargy might be a more appropriate word. God is love. And love is impatient: it is we who, by our failure to respond to the promptings of the Spirit, force God to be 'patient'. As to those who say that visible unity is impossible, the Cardinal has his own answer: 'What is difficult can be done at once, what is impossible takes a little longer'.

Cardinal Suenens discovered charismatic renewal in the United States. From there he brought it to Europe. In his own Belgium it is always before his eyes and in his heart. He has presided at gatherings on the Continent, in England and in Ireland. In September 1975 he attended a Charismatic Congress in Dublin at which catholics and protestants from the Irish Republic and from Ulster worshipped together.

What does charismatic renewal mean to the Cardinal personally?

We have the testimony both of others and of himself.

In his relations with others he has become more relaxed than formerly, more at ease. As well as participating in prayer groups, he has learnt to pray informally in day to day encounters and, in so doing, gives joy to many – and, to the troubled and faint-hearted, reassurance.

'To pray together in this way', he says, 'is completely different from repeating a "ready-made" prayer. I began to understand the freedom of God's children in the presence of the Lord. This does not mean we should not observe and respect at the same time the traditional norms for the liturgy.'

He learnt to pray when receiving, perhaps, a visitor or presiding at a meeting. At first he found it a little embarrassing. 'I still need courage', he writes, 'to ask someone to pray with me, perhaps to open the Bible together and pray to the Lord for light. As I began to do this, whether it was to ask for guidance on a decision we had to take or simply to praise and thank God together, I felt shy and awkward. Only an act of faith in the presence of Jesus in our midst, more real than ourselves, made this possible for me.'

As when participating in the Vatican Council and the Synods, he had to overcome his natural shyness. This needed courage, and he has courage.

In April 1976, Cardinal Suenens was awarded the Templeton Foundation Prize for Progress in Religion.

He received it on Monday April 12 from Prince Philip, Duke of Edinburgh, at Buckingham Palace.

*Excerpts from the Writings of
Cardinal Suenens*

ABBREVIATIONS

1. THE FATHER, THE SON AND THE HOLY SPIRIT

Our Father

We know that God is our Father.

We say in the Lord's Prayer: 'Our Father who art in heaven'.

But do we really believe that God is a father: that there is no father like him, that all fatherhood proceeds from him, takes its title from him?

Do we grasp the meaning, the warmth, the fulness contained in the word 'Father'? Modern man finds it hard to accept the fatherhood of God. He is haunted by the picture, presented by science, of man hurtling through space in a satellite, lost in the immensity of the universe. He feels he is a speck of dust, a drop in the ocean, an ant in an ant-hill. Conscious of how small he is, he is tempted to believe that he is too small, too microscopic, too insignificant, for God to take notice of him.

Is it possible, we ask, that God cares for each one of us as a father cares; loves each of us as a father loves? Yes, God loves us as though each

31

were the only person on earth, for we are brothers of Christ, sons of the same Father.

C.L.D.D.

God knows each one of us. He does not confuse one with the other.

He knows us by name.

He knows the story of our life, page by page, line by line, between the lines, even the water-mark on the paper.

He is with us step by step, from the cradle to the grave. The hairs of our head are numbered.

He is the Father who in the Gospel goes out to meet the prodigal son. He does not wait for his son to speak words of sorrow: he reaches out his arms to him.

God loves us and keeps us in all our ways.

He has given his angels charge over us. He has numbered all our bones.

ibid.

Our God is a hidden God

His love for us is a hidden love.

When the disciples saw Jesus walking on the water, they thought he was a ghost.

When Mary Magdalene saw her risen Master, she thought he was the gardener.

32

The disciples who met Jesus on the road to Emmaus, mistook him for a stranger.

God is concealed in chance happenings, unexpected encounters, secondary causes. We must look beyond appearances.

Bristol 1973

God loves you: I have nothing more wonderful to say to you.

ibid.

Ordinary and extraordinary . . .

In the sight of God there is no line of demarcation between 'ordinary' and 'extraordinary'. He crosses with ease the dotted line that marks our frontiers. In God the extraordinary is ordinary.

God does not love us with ordinary love, making exceptions from time to time. No, the extraordinary love of God is part of his being: our God is wonderful, prodigal in his love for man. The most astonishing proofs of this love – the Incarnation the Eucharist, the Cross – surpass anything we could imagine. Scripture tells us quite simply: 'God so loved the world that he gave his only son . . .' (Jn 3 16). This unbelievable love, welling up from the depths of his heart, overflows upon mankind.

N.P.

Christ, the heart of the world . . .

Christ is the heart of the world: the life-centre which gives to it its reality, subsistence, and direction. In his letter to the Colossians St Paul, quoting an ancient hymn, speaks of Christ as the 'image of the unseen God, the first-born of all creation, for in him were created all things in heaven and on earth . . . all things were created through him and for him. Before anything was created, he is and he holds all things in unity. For the Church is his body and he is its head.' (Col 1 15–18).

F.C.C.

There is only one world. There are not two: one natural, the other supernatural. The only world is that in which we are created, redeemed, and sanctified in Jesus Christ. Creation is not a profane reality. It is a christian reality the dimensions of which lie open to the gaze of faith.

ibid.

In Christ the world has not only been created, but re-created. St Gregory Nazianzen, in a Christmas sermon, speaks of the Nativity of

Christ as a 'festival of re-creation'. The birth of Christ, although an historical event, is not an end, but a means to the renewal, sanctification, and re-creation of the universe. We commemorate not so much the birth of a child as the ultimate transfiguration of man and the whole created world.

In the Byzantine liturgy this view of Christmas is echoed:

Your Nativity, O Christ, our God, has shed the light of knowledge upon the world. Those who had been star-worshippers learned through a star to worship you, O Sun of Justice, and to recognise in you the one who rises and who comes from on high. O Lord, to you be glory!

And:

Your coming, O Christ, has shed upon us a great light. O Light of Light, Radiance of the Father, you have illumined the entire creation!

ibid.

The humanity of Christ . . .

We are discovering more and more the genuine humanity of Christ. We cannot, it is true, remain on that level only, for Christ is both fully human and fully divine. There is a temptation to think about Christ as 'fifty-fifty': partially human, partly divine. That is not so. He is completely human, completely divine. Or, again, we think of his being human in spite of his divinity. No, he is human because of his divinity. His humanity is so human that it is transcendentally human; and he is human in a unique way, because he is the unique Son of God.

That is how it is. You feel that Christ, only, is completely human: so human that he makes you realise you are not human enough yourself.

New York 1972

The Gospel is profoundly human; Jesus knows the heart of man. At his first meeting with Nathanael, the Master said he had seen him under the fig tree. Nathanael was astonished. Whereupon Jesus promised that he would see yet greater things. For Jesus, evidently, the night of faith is not pitch darkness, devoid of stars. We should take to heart sayings scattered through the Gospels, in which he promises 'a peace which the world cannot give' (Jn 14 27) and a joy that 'no man can take from you' (Jn 16 22).

The Lord did not promise that his disciples would be without suffering. On the contrary, he stressed the need to take up one's cross and follow him. But even so, he promised peace and joy. Hence, the serenity to which the disciples bear witness; they learnt from experience that 'his yoke is easy and his burden light'. They knew also the truth of his words: 'Whoever loves me will be loved by my Father and I shall love him and reveal myself to him' (Jn 14 21).

N.P.

Exhausted, Jesus sat by the well of Jacob. A woman of Samaria came, carrying a pitcher. What could be more simple? And yet what an encounter between God's mercy and the frailty of man! By the conversation that ensued the woman's life was changed. Rescued from her past, she proclaimed to her people the coming of the Messiah.

C.L.D.D.

If any man thirst . . .

The humanity of Jesus was penetrated by the Holy Spirit; he was guided by the Spirit at every stage of his life, up to his supreme act of love: death on the Cross. And this same Spirit he promised to his own to continue his work:

> 'If any man thirst, let him come to me! Let him who believes in me come and drink!'
> As the Scripture says: 'From his breast shall flow fountains of living water.'

N.P.

A priest, in trouble, came to me one day and said: 'I want to ask you, as my Bishop just one question. What does Christ mean to you, personally? There is nothing else I want to ask – just that'.

And so I spoke from the depths of my heart. I told him that for me, Christ was the meaning of life, the light of life; that his words give life, joy, hope, peace; that even in the midst of unimaginable suffering he is peace – the expression, indeed the incarnation, of God's love for mankind.

New York 1972

Anointed by the Holy Spirit ...

Jesus and the Holy Spirit are indissolubly united. The name 'Christ' means 'Anointed by the Holy Spirit': indeed the whole life of Jesus reveals the presence within him of the Spirit. The radiance of this presence shone forth when, at his baptism in the river Jordan, the Spirit came down upon him in the form of a dove. The presence of the Spirit manifests itself at times of special significance. The Spirit led him into the wilderness, filled him with jubilation and prayer, inspired in him the love whereby he was subject to the Father's will and, having died and risen from the dead, became for us the 'source of eternal salvation' (Heb 5 9).

N.P.

The Holy Spirit speaks to us not only in the silence of prayer. He speaks through the whole of history, to each generation in a new language. To ours he speaks through a prodigious enrichment in human knowledge: through the anguished searching and groping of man confronted with problems which surpass any known before. We tremble when we think of the possible consequences of power released by nuclear energy and atomic bombs.

The Spirit, known or unknown, is within our every effort to bring among men greater light, sincerity, understanding, peace. St Ambrose taught that whatever is true, no matter by whom it is said, comes from the Holy Spirit.

N.P.

The fruits of the Spirit ...

St Paul speaks of the fruits of the Spirit. Love, joy, peace, patience, kindness, goodness, trust, gentleness, self-control. These are the signs of genuine Christianity. The Spirit bestows such fruits on all who are truly open to him, whether they know him by name or not: 'Your love shines upon us, like the sun at midday'. In a Christian who is faithful to the Spirit, this love, joy, and peace have a unique quality; an intensity that, to those who have eyes to see, reveals a hidden Presence.

N.P.

The Giver and the gifts . . .

St Augustine wrote: 'Not your gifts O Lord but you yourself'. The gifts are no more than the shining rays of the Spirit who is himself the Gift *par excellence,* the Gift who contains all other gifts within him. We must abide with this Spirit, as a person, in his living and radiant reality. The manifestations of the Spirit are the workings of the Holy Spirit. This action or movement of God is infinitely subtle, discreet, and supremely free. The Spirit blows how, when, and where he wills. The gifts are related to the Giver as are its rays to the sun: they are not to be identified with him, but neither have they substance apart from him.

N.P.

The light of the Spirit . . .

To penetrate the secrets of nature requires power-

40

ful, precise instruments. To penetrate the secrets of the presence of God hidden within ourselves and history, we need a power beyond our own. To search out the realm of the invisible we need a light the rays of which are more delicate, more piercing than infra-red. This power, this light, is the Holy Spirit who alone 'explores the depths of God'.

N.P.

We feel more than ever the need to recognise, every one of us, that there is a power much stronger than nuclear energy: the Holy Spirit, the Spirit of Love present among us, guiding mankind.

Address given by Cardinal Suenens on the occasion of being awarded the Templeton Prize.

I believe in the surprises of the Holy Spirit.

Pentecost 1974

The Holy Spirit and Mary

Christianity is a union of two loves in the person of Jesus Christ.

The Holy Spirit is the love of God come down to earth. Mary is human love rising to meet God.

41

Jesus Christ is the heart of this union: the intersection of a two-fold love.

We must try to understand the meaning of this union between the Holy Spirit and his instrument, the Blessed Virgin. We must try to plumb the depths contained in this truth: that Christ is the fruit of this mutual love.

At the heart of the *Credo* are the words: 'And Jesus was incarnate by the Holy Spirit of the Virgin Mary'.

The Trinity

The sign of the Cross bears witness to our belief in the Trinity:

> 'In the name of the Father and the Son and the Holy Spirit'. That is where it all begins; that is where it all ends.

The love of God is there at the beginning: the key to the mystery of creation.

In nomine Patris. 'In the name of the Father'.

What is the good news that we carry to our brethren? That in heaven they have a God who is their Father, who shares with them his life and his riches. There is no more urgent message to proclaim to men. They need to hear it if they are to love one another, for it is in this Fatherhood of God that love has its roots.

'In the name of the Father.'

Do not say that someone is 'unknown' to me. I recognise in him a son of my Father: I am united to him by ties closer than those of blood. I will go to this man; I already know him.

ibid.

'In the name of the Father.'

The Christian will seek out the 'prodigal sons' who have forsaken their home, dissipated their heritage. He will tell them that a place is being kept for them at their Father's table.
'In the name of the Father.'

Let us go about our Father's business. What matters, after all? One thing only; that this Father should communicate with his children, that his glory be made known, his will be done.

ibid.

In nomine Filii 'In the name of the Son'

He overcame the world and asks that we set out with confidence to do the same. Through us, he will do yet greater things than he did himself: that was his promise. 'In the name of the Son.'

He conquered death when he came forth from the tomb on Easter morning: by his death he conquered death. If when we call on his name, (no stone is too heavy to roll away).

43

'In the name of the son.'

He commanded that the Gospel be preached to all men. He promised to be with his Church until the end of time. We believe, therefore, that, beyond all our expectations, God bestows grace in proportion to his commands.

ibid.

In nomine Spiritus Sancti. 'In the name of the Holy Spirit.'

Have we thought of the boldness of the mission which God has entrusted to us; to seek out men, arming ourselves *in Spiritu Sancto,* with the power of his love? To love them not with our feeble love, but with his infinite love – a love which knows no barrier, no limit; which can wait and begin all over again, without growing weary, without taking offence, without expecting the thanks that is due; a love which descends to the abyss of man's destitution yet is unsoiled by contact with what we find repugnant ... A love as strong and as fierce as waves that break against the cliffs, beating with the rhythm of the winds and the tides until the rock crumbles and erodes; a love the gentleness of which surpasses that of a mother.

'In the name of the Holy Spirit'.

We know that Another is working through us, lending us his light and his strength, that the

44

Spirit of God will inspire our thoughts, breathe into our words.

'In the name of the Holy Spirit'.

On Easter morning we cry aloud to the crowd that life has taken on a new meaning since Christ came forth from the tomb and God was reconciled with man.

ibid.

All in all

He is the beginning as he is the end.
He is the Love from whom the world
Came into being.
He is the Love who one day will be
All in all.

ibid.

2. LOVING ONE ANOTHER

Christmas

The feast of Christmas brings before our eyes and awakens in our hearts the central mystery of Christianity: the incarnation of the Son of God; the coming among us of our Saviour.

He chose to be born a child among us, marked from the beginning with the seal of poverty. There was no room for his parents in the inns of Bethlehem crammed already with pilgrims more richly endowed. The angel said to the shepherds, poor among the poor: 'You will find a newly born child wrapped in swaddling clothes, lying in a manger'. All this leaves no doubt as to the preferences, the priorities of God.

Our present economic crisis invites Christians to read the Gospels with new eyes, not that we may find therein ready-made solutions for the complex problems of our times, but that we may derive inspiration which will enable us to work together in solidarity to adopt a new and more humane way of living.

To read afresh in this manner will help us to deepen our faith, to believe that Jesus is in very truth the Saviour because he alone can liberate us from the primary cause of our social evils: the sin of egoism, whether personal or collective, which threatens every society.

In the immediate present the Christian, because he is a Christian, must be ready to co-operate with all men of goodwill in solidarity and sacrifice.

Christmas invites us to a greater awareness of God's preference for the poor: to understand, as does Mary in the Magnificat, that God is on the side of the humble and weak; that he exalts them, that his compassion extends from age to age to all who turn to him in need.

There are different kinds of poverty. There are different kinds of hunger and thirst. The most obvious is that which undermines, destroys the body. It is more difficult to see in a neighbour's home the hidden distress which insists upon keeping up appearances, concealing the hardships imposed by an inadequate budget. And there are other forms of poverty; those which conceal spiritual and moral affliction. Many are those around us who hunger for a little attention, a little concern; who want to be listened to, to know that they are appreciated, accepted. Christmas invites us to be specially attentive to the words of the Master in which he shows once and for all what it

means to be a genuine Christian: 'I was hungry
and you fed me'.

From Pastoralia, December 1975.

You shall love . . .

God said: 'You shall love . . . '

God's entire law is contained in the words:
'You shall love . . . '

This love moves in two directions: towards God
and towards our neighbour. Yet it is one love, not
two. *Duo praecepta, sed una caritas:* two com-
mandments motivated by a single love.

Love extends in concentric circles to the ends of
the earth, from a next-door neighbour to a
neighbour in a distant land. Yet it is one love.

Love's manifestation extends from the union
between husband and wife to a greeting exchang-
ed with a passer-by. Love is a variation on a single
theme.

'You shall love . . .' The words shine like the
star that lead the Magi.

'See how they love one another!' So said the
crowds in Jerusalem when they saw the early
Christians.

L.C.

The love of God in the heart of man . . .

Charity is the love of God dwelling in the heart of man, enlarging it, giving it an unexpected power and capacity. God loves within us and through us.

To love others for the love of God is not enough: this can become artificial. Our hearts need to be sustained not simply by the love of God from without, but transfigured from within.

We are called upon to love others not only *for* the love of God but *with* the love with which God loves them: human love has to take on the properties of God's own love.

How does God love? He takes the initiative. He says the first word.

God's love does not depend on our response. God loves us, if I may so put it, without respite. If we loved our fellowmen with the love of God, we would love them first, we would love them last, we would love them· faithfully, regardless of their response. Our love would take the initiative; it would be unwearying.

C.L.D.D.

The need for love . . .

Human beings seem to be pursuing diverse, complicated ends. They engage in business or politics, art or literature, plough the soil or sail the seas.

Yet behind these facades they are in search of something extremely simple, moving in its simplicity. They are in search of love. They long to love and to be loved.

We all know homes where members of the family live side by side as if they were in a boarding house. They sit at the same table, yet they are strangers to one another.

If you want to bring a little warmth into such a milieu, you must kindle a little warmth in your own heart. You must share more than bread – your heart and your life. We are chary about allowing others to intrude, too ready to shut ourselves away, whether it be timidity, shyness, or resentment. People manage to live in a spiritual isolation, like hermits, when the greatest happiness they could bestow would be to reveal to others their real selves. When you get to know someone intimately it is amazing what an unexpected world comes to light, how different is his outlook from what you imagined, and usually, how full he is of goodwill.

ibid.

Openness . . .

Openness to God is synonymous with openness to the world of men which God has created, loved, and sanctified. To love God is to enter into the mystery of God wherein he so loved us that he gave his only begotten Son who, in turn, left us his commandment that we love one another.

N.P.

Let us not be like those of whom Péguy said: 'They think they love God because they do not love anyone!'

L.C.

In the world of today the idea of 'civilisation' is too often equated with progress seen solely in terms of comfort, prosperity, and power.

It is high time we rejected this inadequate interpretation and stressed the fundamental place of religion in the development of mankind, so that we can measure by a true hierarchy of values all that is human.

Address given by Cardinal Suenens on the occasion of his being awarded the Templeton Prize.

Every time we affirm belief in a Supreme Being who is both immanent and transcendent, in a love which is open to all men and embraces the entire universe, we find ourselves confronted with the very foundation of human society, the basis of all peace and brotherhood among men.

ibid.

Thought for others ...

Charity comprises tact. It senses what others want, for what it is they are waiting. The first miracle, at the wedding feast at Cana of Galilee, came about because the Blessed Virgin had sensed the embarrassment of the hosts who had run short of wine.

C.L.D.D.

A priest in Brussels was coming out of his church when he noticed one of his parishioners, who did not 'practise', taking a photograph of his wife and baby in the porch. He went up to the man and said: 'Don't you think the snap would be nicer if you were in it, too?' There were murmurs of appreciation, and the priest took the snapshot and handed back the camera.

He had gone only a few yards when he heard someone running behind him. He turned. It was the wife. 'Father,' she said, 'my little boy hasn't been christened. Would you baptize him? Contact was made. They talked. The marriage, it turned out, was not valid. One thing led to another. The child was baptized, the marriage regularized. A small, spontaneous act of kindness brought the Christian religion, in all its fulness, into a home.

ibid.

Virtus ex illo exibat . . .

To bring God to others, we must ourselves draw near to them. And this calls for delicacy, sympathy, gentleness, a self-effacement which leaves room for grace, enabling Christ within us to touch hearts: 'Goodness went out from him'.

We should approach others in a spirit of respect, self-forgetfulness – not as a superior, an inferior; an equal, an unequal; but rather as a servant, a master.

Reflect upon what the fox, in Antoine de Saint-Exupéry's *Le Petit Prince,* calls 'taming'. That is, preparing the way to confidence and harmony. A single contact is not enough: we must create a friendly atmosphere, contrive a gradual yielding, prepare a further meeting. All is possible if we have the humility to realise that it is not ourselves but Christ, in and through us, who knocks on the door, not once but again and again. And our exchanges must not be soliloquies nor two monologues, one succeeding the other, but neither replying. We must learn how to listen.

G.E.C.

Forgetfulness of self: Pope John XXIII . . .

To love others is to forget self. Forgetfulness of self conditions the gift of self.

John XXIII, in his own eyes, did not exist. He was devoid of vanity. A fundamental humility allowed him to speak of himself with detachment and humour, as if about someone else.

On becoming Patriarch of Venice he introduced himself to his diocese as follows:

'I want to speak to you with complete frankness. You have waited my coming with impatience. People have talked to you and written to you in a way that far surpasses my deserts. I introduce myself as I really am. Like everyone else on this earth, I come from a particular family, a particular place. Thank God, I have good health and sufficient common sense to allow me to see things quickly and clearly. Ever disposed to love people I abide by the law of the Gospel, respecting my own rights and those of others: this prevents me from harming anyone and encourages me to do good to all.

'I come of lowly stock. I was brought up in the kind of poverty which, if it is limiting, is beneficial: it demands little but guarantees the development of the noblest and greatest qualities, thus preparing one to ascend the steep moun-

tain of life. Providence brought me out of my
native village and caused me to travel both in the
East and the West. The same Providence brought
me on close terms with men differing both in
religion and ideology.

'God confronted me with acute, formidable
social problems in the midst of which I main-
tained a calm, a balanced judgment, as well as
imagination, so as to evaluate things with discern-
ment. Regardful always of Christian belief and
moral principles, I was preoccupied not with
what separates people and provokes conflict, but
with what unites them'.

Homily delivered in commemoration of Pope
John XXIII. October 23rd 1963

After the death of John XXIII an agnostic
friend of mine said to me: 'Pope John has made
my lack of belief uncomfortable'.

Malines 1973

Respect . . .

One day the late King Albert of the Belgians,
before going down a coal-mine, asked a miner if
there was anything he wanted for himself or his
comrades. The reply was proud and unequivocal:
'Sire, we want others to respect us'. It was a cry

from the heart. Most of all, men want respect.

C.L.D.D.

People are usually better at heart than they seem to be and appreciate being treated accordingly.

ibid.

Christianity entails a respect for man that is inseparable from faith in a God who is infinitely good and the Father of us all.

For the Christian, the affirmation of God does not detract from the greatness of man, nor does faith in God alienate us from our brothers.

Respect for man, or the recognition of man by man, has its origin in the recognition of man by God. The psalmist, addressing God, cries:

What is man that you are mindful of him?
You have made him a little lower than the
  angels.
You have crowned him with glory and honour.
You have given him dominion over the works of
  your hands.
You have put all things under his feet (Ps 81
67)

In conferring upon each of us a dignity which transcends all the blessings of this earth, and upon life an infinite value, Christianity has proved to be inestimably fruitful in humanising us. It has fostered a respect for life and for death, a realisation of the equality of each one of us, a love of truth and truthfulness (a plain 'Yes' or 'No' is all you need to answer, the Gospel tells us). It maintains an elevated concept of liberty and responsibility, gentleness in human relations, a sense of proportion, a repugnance for fanaticism, the priority of work over money, fidelity in love, and the sanctity of the family.

C.C.

Christianity's awareness of man is not in the nature of an abstract ideology or a pleasant feeling of universal sympathy devoid of contact with reality. It is the soul and driving force of action. The essential truth of Christianity is in the words of the scriptures: 'If a man loves not the brother he has seen, how can he love God whom he has not seen?' And again: 'If a man has enough to live on, yet, when he sees his brother in need, closes his heart against him, how can we say that the love of God dwells in him?'

Of the bond uniting love of God and the service of one's brethren: Bernanos says 'What others expect of us, God expects of us'.

ibid.

Listening . . .

We must listen not only to what is said but to what is not said. Few of us can take in the meaning of an awkward silence, a hint, a word unspoken. We listen to words and sounds, but have no ear for mute distress or half-confidences diffidently offered.

We must even realise that sometimes a 'no' can conceal a 'yes'. Our Lady at the marriage at Cana, when she asked her Son to intervene, received an apparently negative answer. Nevertheless she turned to the servants, bidding them be ready. She had heard more than the spoken word.

C.L.D.D.

There are splendid listeners who have the gift of getting others to talk. By encouraging them, expecting much of them, they bring out what is best — make them even surpass themselves. Listeners of this quality are rare, but more than one writer has, we know, found his greatest inspiration and enthusiasm in the affection and companionship of a wife who shares her husband's life.

ibid.

Deterioration in morals

The deterioration in public morality has been denounced both by Cardinal Marty, Archbishop of Paris, and by Georges Marchais, leader of the Communist Party in France. This sharing of views does not happen every day: it makes one think.

But to react is not enough. Positive education and guidance are needed both in the family and in the school, if we are to inculcate respect for basic human values, among which love comes first. If yesterday we spoke of love as if sex were non-existent, today it is the reverse. The obsession with sex explains the popularity of pornographic films from which love – in the true sense of the word – is totally excluded. It is even claimed that freedom from all moral constraint is a remedy that can heal the misery and sexual unfulfilment of contemporary men and women.

And the most startling aspect of all is the fact that we are participating in the 'desacralisation' of the greatest of all realities: human love; love that is, which is genuinely human and authentic. Recently a writer condemned the present flood of pornography in an article he appropriately entitled 'The Assassins of Love'.

Love (this cannot be said too often) is sacred because it is created in the image of God who is himself love.

What I have said is true for every human being, whether a Christian or not. For the Christian new perspectives and dimensions open up. He has a special reason for being on the alert, on the watch, concerning responsibilities both negative and positive. His faith tells him that human love is implanted in his very being by the love of the living God who vivifies this from within. This Presence is for him a source that is for ever gushing forth, for ever new in its life and its richness.

From Pastoralia October '75

Responsibility . . .

'To be a man' Antoine de Saint-Exupéry writes, 'is, in brief, to be responsible.'

To define man in terms of his responsibility before the bar of history is to define the man of our times whom we must educate both within ourselves and among those around us, so that he may prove himself worthy to live in the human family on a global scale. The development of this sense of responsibility is the great task of our century. It is a task both spiritual and moral from which none is entitled to exempt himself – least of all the Church.

C.L.D.D.

Liberty of public opinion within the Church is right, but it implies the responsibility of exercising this in faith and charity. We must be on our guard against both mute servility and unbridled criticism.

C.C.

Berdyaeff said that Communism is the outcome of neglect on the part of Christ's followers; a sign of Christian responsibility disregarded. We must beat our breasts in shame: 'O you of little faith, why did you doubt?' We saw before us mountains of prejudice, animosity, bitterness and we did not believe, with a living faith, that we could move these mountains.

G.E.C.

We must not accuse Satan before we ourselves plead guilty.

ibid.

Lacordaire defined the Christian as 'a man to whom Jesus Christ confided other men'. These men confided to us are not men of yesterday, but of here and now: our neighbours we meet in the street, our companions at work, our young people.

London 1970

We must face the problem posed by the gap
between rich and poor nations – in particular the
failure of the rich to help the poor. We must not
by-pass this responsibility as the Pharisee and the
Levite by-passed the Samaritan on the road to
Jericho.

The Catholic Voice. California 1968

We are inclined to think that our charity is all it
should be, because, as we see it, we do no harm to
anyone. We find it hard to grasp that there is a sin
against charity: the sin of omission or, in the
words of Léon Bloy: 'the crime of not loving'.

C.L.D.D.

Only the Holy Spirit can teach us to spread the
Gospel, while at the same time respecting
another's freedom of conscience.

Christ never said 'Force people to be converts,'
but 'Offer the Good News in a spirit of freedom
and joy'.

When we possess something that gives us joy
we reveal spontaneously our desire to share this.
When I say to someone: 'Look, there is the dawn',
I do not constrain him to raise his eyes. I'm not

63

forcing him. I'm offering him a deeper experience of joy.

New York 1970

Women . . .

If as Lenin said, 'a revolution without the support of women is unthinkable,' they are no less necessary for the establishment of peace. Women of the world, we need you!

United Nations, New York 1963

Women should be invited to the Vatican Council as auditors. Unless I am mistaken, they make up one half of the human race.

Second Vatican Council, 1963

In the past, woman was imprisoned within a framework of an idealized archtype established by man. She was expected to be docile, resigned, faithful (this within clearly defined limits) protected from the world: Penelope at her weaving; Margaret at her spinning-wheel; Juliet on her balcony. Today the independence of woman is a *fait accompli*. She no longer acts solely through her influence on man, but in her own right.

N.W.

The up-dating of nuns . . .

'Don't leave one poor cardinal to do all the fighting for you! It's your battle.'
Boston 1964. Address to Religious.

The role of woman is, I believe, complementary to that of man not only in the home, but in the social and political sphere in its various aspects. An Arabian proverb says: 'Men see the forest, women the trees and the leaves'. I think this is true. We need two eyes to see things in their true perspective, one is not enough.

It is much the same here; women have an awareness of values which men often allow themselves to overlook or simply do not see. Men are easily tempted to reduce reality to concepts. Moreover, they usually take the lead in the world of industry, technology, scientific discovery. This is their greatness, but it is also their limitation.

This complementary role of woman ought to be given full scope within the Church, too, at a variety of levels. I am not saying this *necessarily* includes the priesthood. That is another story. We must realise that it is, to say the least, a complex one raising problems which will not simply be solved just at the whim of popular feeling.

65

Women are already occupied with vast areas of human activity and they will take their place more and more. Their creative gifts find expression particularly in the field of education, in human relationships and in all that concerns personal life and the ethical issues of the day. 'The crowning glory of love' it has been said, 'is intuition'. Many needs still require to be satisfied if the world is to be made a better place in which to live. There is a place for the intuitions of the heart in a world which has a desperate need to find its soul.

Malines 1976

The Young . . .

The young deserve our attention. Their total questioning invites us to reflect.

The Gospel as proclaimed by, for instance, the 'Jesus Movement' or the 'Jesus Freaks' is not complete. Theirs is not the Jesus of mature faith: often the divine dimension is lacking. In spite of these defects the young seek in Jesus a reason for hope, a means of freeing themselves from many kinds of slavery: in a morally polluted atmosphere they look for air.

Robert Kennedy used to say that the tragedy of the young in America lay in the fact that they had everything except one only: a reason for living.

To find in Jesus Christ an ultimate purpose for living they must see in us a Gospel which is alive.

This is a grave hour for the Church. In the nineteenth century we lost the working classes. In the twentieth are we going to lose the young?

N.P.

Negative education is as bad as no education.

The young do not want to be told what they cannot or may not do, but how to develop what is best, what is generous within them. Youth, Claudel said, craves not simply enjoyment but heroism.

L.C.

Many of the young would have done better at school and at home if the praise given to them had been less sparing.

How did we learn to ride a bicycle? Were we not lifted into the saddle, supported, told again and again not to be alarmed – to look straight ahead. All would be well, we were told: we were nearly there . . . we were there!

The sun makes the flowers open: cold and darkness close them. Encouragement brings people out, cheers them. It is a form of charity that is within the reach of us all.

Criticism to do good must be constructive. Few

can resist the eroding effect of negative criticism. Few have the courage, enthusiasm, and humour to go on in the face of disapproval.

C.L.D.D.

The young think the world began on the day they were born, just as the old think it will end when they die!

London 1971

Parents and teachers should co-operate, for they are concerned with the same adolescents, the same adults of tomorrow. Their efforts are interwoven, the tasks they share will have a single outcome.

L.C.

Youth in the home . . .

In the family we speak in words, but we say more by the atmosphere we create – tone of voice, the use of certain expressions, a thousand unnoticed things. The life that parents share is, in the watchful eyes of their adolescent children, a fundamental, indispensable object lesson. The young throughout life will carry in their hearts a picture of their parents. And if it is a favourable one, love

will mean for them living in harmony, with un-
concealed affection – as did their father and
mother.

ibid.

There is one saviour only: Jesus Christ. The
young, disillusioned with a materialistic society,
use his name: today I saw scrawled on a car the
words 'Jesus loves you'. Perhaps those who wrote
them do not understand all that the name implies.
Perhaps, like John the Baptist, they proclaim that
in our midst there is one whom we do not know.

Cambridge 1973

I hope [the young] will thrust us forward. They
will have to learn that some form of institutional
Church is needed. You cannot have a soul
without a body; this is the logic of the Incarnation. But they let in fresh air – a feeling of spring,
a verve. I hope they will bring us nearer to Christ.
If we come nearer to Christ the rest will follow.
We do not first love the Church. Because of Christ
we love the Church which brings us Christ and
his Gospel.

Interview, Malines 1972

Some ecumenical thoughts . . .

During Vatican II a symbol of the bond between
West and East was provided in the *aula* by the
chair of Peter supported by the Latin Fathers, St
Augustine and St Ambrose and the Greek
Fathers, St Athanasius and St John Chrysostom.
Moreover the Eastern prelates participating in
the Council helped us to find again 'the absent
half of ourselves'. In addition they were a symbol
of all non-European churches. Their voice was an
appeal to us to recognize the fact that the sister
churches of Asia, Africa and Latin America are
capable, as are the churches of Europe to assume
their own character and their individual struc-
tures. We realised too, that recognition of diversi-
ty could have important repercussions when the
question of the Anglican and other Christian
churches came to the fore.

C.C.

An Orthodox theologian asked at the Vatican
Council what he thought was the main obstacle to
reunion between the orthodox church and the
church of Rome, replied: 'the fact, that we have
not spoken to one another for nine centuries'.

ibid.

The Lord, with an 'impatient patience', urges

us on to hasten the day of visible unity among all Christians. We are well aware of this. Unity, however, will not come about solely through discussions between men of goodwill, any more than it will be the fruit of a diplomatic compromise. The foundation of union one with another is at a much deeper level. It must be sought in the heart and truth of God himself: the unity we seek will evolve from spiritual renewal and from unceasing prayer offered up together.

Address given by Cardinal Suenens on the occasion of the award of the Templeton Prize

Reconciliation between the different Christian bodies will not come through high-level discussions between the Church of Rome and the Church of Istanbul, the Church of Rome and the Church of Moscow, the Church of Rome and the Church of Canterbury. Such discussions must continue, but the final solution will be the consequence of our searching together to be united with the same Christ, the same Spirit. If all the Christian Churches follow the same path in search of Christ and allow Christ to unite them through himself, then unity will come. If I cannot name the day or the moment, I can be certain that the Spirit of God is at work.

London 1976

Prayer in common, sustained by the Word of God is an unfailing spring at which Christians of every denomination can gather and quench their thirst in an atmosphere of mutual respect and love.

N.P.

A dream

Like anyone else, I dream dreams. I dream of a day when a Second Council of Jerusalem will be held in the city of the *cenaculum* – the city that is the cradle of the Church: that participating at it along with the Pope will be the Patriarch of Constantinople and the Primate of All England.

London 1972

Let us eliminate from our conversation anything that keeps men apart, estranges them, sets up a barrier, exaggerates differences and divergencies, wounds them.

Let us foster what brings people together. Let us have the courage to be peacemakers.

London 1976

'There was a man sent from God whose name was John'. When Pope John received the observers at Vatican II he spoke to them in plain, simple words. 'We do not intend,' he said, 'to conduct a trial of the past; we do not want to prove who was right or who was wrong; the faults were on both sides. All we want to say is: 'Let us come together. Let us put an end to our divisions.' And he used to say: 'Some people want to complicate simple matters. I want to simplify complicated ones'. And he also said: 'I don't know where we are going. Let us simply follow day by day whatever the Holy Spirit asks of us'.

Malines 1972

3. THE CHURCH

The Church is a supernatural mystery of communion.

The Church is a supernatural mystery the roots of which are in eternity.

The Church is a reality of the past, an actuality of the present, an openness to the future.

C.C.

The Church in History

The Church is a reality situated within history. The moment in which we live is better understood if we link it both to yesterday and tomorrow, just as, in plotting the position of a ship, we must calculate the latitude and longitude on the map. If we understand the Church in relation to time in general we will be better able to understand it in relation to our own time. We cannot but profit by viewing the Church as being at the heart of history, and not as an abstract reality immutable and outside time.

E.F.T.

To maintain continuity with the past is for the Church a primary duty. From the past the Church draws its sap, its source of life. The Church's earliest origin is to be found in the history of Israel; in company with the people of the Old Covenant it travels back through the centuries. The Church has never allowed itself to be severed from its Jewish past. When the Fathers of the Second Vatican Council made a declaration favourable to the Jews, this was not simply a matter of justice: it was the expression of the Church's fidelity to itself.

ibid.

In the context of the Church, history teaches us humility and confidence: humility because history shows that we carry our treasures in earthen vessels; confidence because we are able to see God at work in the Church, despite its human inadequacy. Gamaliel, we read in the Acts of the Apostles, said to the tribunal which wanted to condemn Peter and John: 'If this enterprise, this movement of theirs, is human in origin, it will disintegrate; but if it comes from God you will not only be unable to destroy it – you will find yourselves fighting against God'.

ibid.

Our daily bread . . .

God, the Book of Exodus shows us, does not give
to his people lavish provisions for their journey:
he gives us enough manna for each day as it
comes. We have become accustomed to ac-
cumulating cumbersome accessories; houses of
stone and cement instead of tents that can be fold-
ed and carried, enabling us at a moment's notice
to take up our journey afresh.

ibid.

The Church and the Eucharist

The reality of the Church is like that of the
Eucharist. The two mysteries are related. If the
Church makes the Eucharist, the Eucharist
makes the Church.

The Eucharist is at the same time a memorial
of the past; a present actualisation of the unique
sacrifice offered by Christ once and for all; an an-
ticipation of the resurrection. It is, therefore,
memorial, actualisation, prophesy.

The Eucharist has remained the same down the
ages, giving unchangeable expression to itself in
words that recall the Master until he comes.

Unessentials have varied. The Eucharist has

been celebrated in many liturgies: Aramaic, Greek. Latin, Slavonic, Coptic, Chaldaean, and, in our own day, in the vernacular the world over. It has been accompanied by Gregorian chant, polyphony, and now the music of any number of peoples – thus becoming all things to all men. Its prayers have been framed in the balanced classical phrases of Rome. It has taken to itself the lyricism and exuberance of the East. It acknowledges, too, the need to adjust to the taste of modern man.

Equally, the Upper Room, without losing its identity, has given place to an altar of a martyr in the catacombs, a villa of a patrician convert, a basilica of Constantine, a Roman church, a Gothic or Baroque cathedral, an unpretentious modern church. Always the same Eucharist, it finds expression in a liturgy that is faithful to the past and open to the future.

C.C.

Christians?

Are we, in truth, what our name signifies? One with Christ? Do we open ourselves so as to be possessed by him, so that we can say in truth: 'I am not living. Christ is living in me, loving in me, speaking through me, coming and going through me.'? We cannot have a Eucharist without bread and wine. We cannot have a baptism without water. So, also, Christ cannot live his life today in this world without our mouths, without our eyes, without our comings and goings without our hearts. He desires to love through our hearts. When we love, he is loving through us. This is Christianity.

New York 1972

Co-responsibility

The sense of co-responsibility among Christians has been awakened. There remains, however, some distance to travel before all the consequences can be disentangled. But a beginning has been made which will grow. This is the moment to call to mind the words of Victor Hugo: 'There is nothing more powerful than an idea the hour of which has come'. For good or ill a new way of life is emerging in the Church.

E.F.T.

It is easier to give orders than to call forth real co-operation. It is easier to do something for another than to do it with him, to solve a problem than to enable another to do so for himself. It is essential that a priest should not assume an

79

authoritarian stance: he must trust the laity, resist the temptation to do everything himself.

G.E.C.

The priest because he is the servant of all is entitled to co-operation from others.

Address to priests at Chur, Switzerland, 1969

'With you I am one of the faithful, for you I am a bishop.'

A saying from St Augustine
quoted in the same address.

The exercise of authority

Those in authority, inside and outside the Church, need the entire backing of the community if they are to exercise their function. In the process of decision making they need the co-operation of all. The image of authority is changing, which does not mean that authority is no longer necessary. It does mean that it shows greater respect in relation to the individual. The leader is no longer the man who has all the answers – he is the man who can create an environment in which discussion, research, and constructive criticism are possible, and in which answers emerge by a gradual process of consent. This, I think, is the direction in which the Church of the future will move – all sections together through, with, and under authority.

Interview (N.C.R.) 9.3.69

The role of the priest . . .

The priest is called upon to enter into Christ's mission in relation to his Father and to all mankind. He cannot reduce this mission purely to an earthly dimension; the Church is not a spiritual Red Cross nor is the priest a social worker. He is committed at one and the same time to the second commandment, to love one's neighbour, and to the first which requires of us an awareness and adoration of God.

Address at Chur.

We are the Church, all of us . . .

We are too inclined to speak about the Church as something outside us. We criticize the Church: we say the Church should do this or do that, should have done this or that, forgetting that we ourselves are the Church, all of us together.

New York 1972

81

The Church is not a democracy. The reality is much deeper. We are the people of God; but when you speak in human terms of 'people' you tend to think of 'people' in opposition to 'government'. Now when you speak of the People of God in the Church, you mean all the baptized children of God. Pope, bishops, and laity, we are all of us, the baptized children of God. And once we stress this truth about the people of God we are more correctly understood as living in close communion – not as a people in opposition to their leaders.

ibid.

The Church is for the world. It must overcome its inner tensions so as to be able better to fulfil its mission in relation to all men and the problems that confront them.

Interview 1969

Freedom of Speech . . .

There is a great liberating force in the honest expression of what one believes to be the truth.

Interview May 1969

82

Frank, open, and constructive discussion, inspired by a love of the Church and its head, is a sign of vitality and strength. It is perfectly natural that there should be this kind of discussion about vital problems concerning the whole Church – all the more so when these problems are felt in their acuteness and urgency the world over and are publicly discussed in the press ... To clamp down on discussion on these differences, on the pretext of preserving unity, seems to me harmful in the present day.

Interview June 1969

We should discover and accept the element of truth in every criticism.

Figaro June 1969

Christians should be open to one another in a spirit of fraternity. No one should consider his opponent as being heretical. We see people doing injury to others in the name of the Gospel. Not one of us possesses the truth in its fulness. I believe that the present crisis is in the nature of a catharsis; I understand the anguish of the Pope and I share it with him.

Paris Match May 69

No one has the right to present himself as the sole defender of the Pope. We all profess the same deference and fidelity. But we should have the courage to recognise our disagreements, if we are not to be bogged down in ambiguity.

Intervention Synod. 1969

Let us believe in the Holy Spirit who, in each of us according to his role, is actively present in the Pope, the theologians, the bishops, and the faithful.

Let us believe in the Holy Spirit who also speaks to us through the signs of the times.

ibid.

Let us have greater confidence in the life-giving action of the Holy Spirit, the principle and the source of unity in the Church.

ibid.

An old priest said to me: 'When I was in the seminary I learnt the answer to every imaginable question.

Unhappily no one asks me these questions.'

New York 1972

Look upon the faith of your Church . . .

Christianity cannot be reduced to an ideology. It is first and foremost an event, a person: Jesus Christ acknowledged as Lord.

A christian is not a philosopher who has opted for an explanation of the universe: he is someone who has experienced in his own life Jesus of Nazareth, crucified on Good Friday, risen from the tomb on Easter Sunday. The cry of Claudel: 'Why, all of a sudden you have become A PERSON!' is a cry of faith for all generations.

E.F.T.

If, however, the christian derives his life from .the past, lives in consequence of a unique event in the past, he does not make contact with that same past across a void of twenty centuries. No, the past comes to him, alive in the Church. In saying to his disciples: 'Behold I am with you always, even to the end of the world', Christ assured them of his presence in the Church. In Christ the past is overcome. Through him and in him the Church comes to us as the heir of a past which is vividly present.

ibid.

The christian of today goes to meet his Lord

not only with his personal faith, but with the faith of the whole Church both of yesterday and today. At the moment of the breaking of the bread the Church puts on our lips the splendid prayer: 'Lord, look not upon our sins but upon the faith of your Church'. It is with this ecclesial faith that I go to meet the Son of God. I believe with the faith of the Patriarchs and Prophets; with the faith of Mary, the Apostles, the martyrs, the doctors, the confessors, the mystics, the saints.

It is a great moment when, during an ordination, we sing the Litany of the Saints, feel ourselves united with our forefathers in the faith, whose mediation we are asking on behalf of the ordinand.

ibid.

No, the Church must not canonise the past. We must guard against 'primitivism', that is, an attempt to keep alive some past century as an ideal or norm. There is no golden age that ought to be restored. We should not have any nostalgia, even for the primitive Church. We must not deceive ourselves: the picture of the earliest christian communities is far from idyllic.

ibid.

Preach the Gospel

'Go, preach the Gospel,' was said not to the Apostles only, but to all who with them and after them share their task. It cuts through time and space, as lightning flashes through the darkness.

G.E.C.

People ask of the Church, whether they realise it or not, that the Gospel be revealed to them. They want to meet the Christ who is alive today; they want to see him with their eyes, touch him with their hands. Like those who approached Philip saying: 'We want to see Jesus', our contemporaries want to see him face to face. They want each of us to reflect Christ, just as a pane of glass reflects the sun.

All that is opaque and besmirched in us disfigures the face of Christ in the Church. The unbeliever reproaches us not because we are christians but because we are not christian enough. That is the tragedy. Gandhi, when he read the Gospel, was impressed: he even thought of becoming a christian. But the christians he met put him off, made him withdraw. So heavy is our responsibility.

E.F.T.

We have to present the living faith, the fulness of the apostolic tradition, to the men of our own day. This can mean having to change our vocabulary: words are living realities and their meanings change. If I were to preach in China instead of in Belgium, I would say that Christ is sitting at the left, not the right, hand of the Father, for in China the left is the place of honour. Also we must pay heed to the cultural, conceptual, and sociological milieu in which the Good News is being proclaimed. We have not only to translate the message, but to transpose it into a different key. Moreover, as the message was first given in a rural setting: we may have to change some of the imagery, make it intelligible to those living in cities. We must try to make our approximations adequate, while bearing in mind that the highest degree of our knowledge of God is 'to understand', St Gregory of Nyssa reminds us, 'that we cannot understand him'.

F.C.C.

The Church of the future

The fact that we are called upon to be guardians of tradition does not mean that we are committed to immobility.

C.C.

We need a Church comprising those who want to belong, in whom the freedom of God's children is so plain to see that being a christian appears to be not the consequence of authoritarian injunctions imposed from without, under pain of mortal sin, but, rather, an imperative felt deep within us, springing up from a source that is the logic of our faith.

N.P.

Each one will have to choose for himself, in full clarity and freedom, whether he wants to have his life animated by Jesus Christ or not. No adult will be able to be a christian by proxy; the decision will rest solely with him and will depend largely on the kind of Christianity he is being offered and which he sees being lived. He will need not only doctrine but living examples.

ibid.

We must give to the christian of tomorrow a faith which is strong and exhilarating; grafted on to the power of the Holy Spirit, protected under the shadow of his wings, performing 'signs and wonders' which attest that we live in that burgeoning of a new life which is Pentecost.

ibid.

An irreversible trend has taken possession of the People of God, filling them with a longing for renewal in their lives: for joy, change, progress, and freedom within the Church of today.

There is an urgent need to give support to this trend, meet it fairly and squarely, so as to be able to direct it.

Malines 1971

What is the Church expecting from the young?

That you go forth, here and now, and proclaim the Good News.

But, we are told, the time is not ripe, people are not ready to listen.

In the time of Jesus were they ready? I do not think so: I have only to look at a crucifix. When Paul at Athens tried to speak about the Resurrection, were they ready? Not at all. 'Most interesting' they said, 'but we're busy. Come back another day.'

If we wait till people are ready we will wait till eternity. Show what it means to be a christian. Open your hearts and your arms to others, in love and joy. That is what the Church and the world are waiting for.

Seventh International Conference on Catholic Charismatic Renewal. Notre Dame, Indiana 1973

To make the future we must have confidence in that future and an understanding of the new generation with their problems, allergies, aspirations, failings. It is with them that we have to construct the future.

Vatican II Anniversary Nov. 1970

When in *Gaudium et Spes* we are asked to 'read the signs of the times' this is not a request that the Church be adapted to current fashions. It is primarily an appeal, with the men of our era in mind, to re-read the Gospel in the light of the Holy Spirit; to absorb afresh the word of God which is always living, always contemporary. Only thus can the Church be open to the "surprises of the Holy Spirit".

E.F.T.

Impatiently patient ...

Much has been said of God's patience. Let us understand this aright. God is love and love is impatient to communicate itself. God is in haste to give himself to man. The slow working of his grace is not willed by him. He wills to give himself today. St Paul's cry 'The love of God constrains us', echoes the divine urgency. God is patient because we compel him to be patient. He is, if we may so put it, impatiently patient: he asks us by our eagerness to translate his impatience into action.

G.E.C.

4. PRAYER AND FAITH

A hunger for God ...

Hidden deep in the heart of man is an immense longing for God.

C.L.D.D.

One day a teacher who was working in a country behind the Iron Curtain asked in an infants' class if anyone would like to recite a poem – any poem.

A little girl put up her hand. She would like, she said, to recite one she repeated every night to her grandmother. She began: 'Our Father who art in heaven ...' The others all joined in.

In a country in which it is forbidden to mention the name of God, faith lives on.

ibid.

Always . . .

We dare to believe in the power of prayer because
we have the example of Jesus. Before he put his
prayer into words, he said to his Father: 'Father, I
thank you for hearing my prayer. I know indeed
that you always hear me' (Jn 11).

ibid.

Confidence . . .

We find it hard to pray with confidence. Often
prayer is an importuning that God should do our
will: an announcement of what we consider needs
to be done (and done quickly). There is no confidence in this, only anxiety and self-centredness.
We have no need to ask God for our happiness.
He never ceases to want it. It is we ourselves who
put obstacles in his way, hold his love in check.
God always hears man's prayer and is himself the
eternal answer.

Our prayers are answered the moment they are
true prayers and to the extent that this is so. And
true prayer is nothing other than opening our
hearts to God. It is summed up in the Apocalypse,
in the appeal: 'Come, Lord Jesus'.

Confidence is not synonymous with certainty
that God will do all I ask. It is a conviction that he
will answer as only he knows how: that is, like a

94

Father whose love is boundless, who knows everything, and will grant me what is best.

The answer may fall short of my expectation, even be contrary to what I want. God loves us infinitely more than we love ourselves. To trust is to believe in his love: to close our eyes, leave all to him.

ibid.

There are times when we walk in darkness, but God sees us, and that is what matters. He does not forsake us. He holds us by the hand, even when we are unaware of it.

ibid.

We are no longer alone if we allow ourselves to be guided by the Holy Spirit. Our life unfolds in response to him. As we dispossess ourselves our being is possessed by God: the void is filled. God who is welcome, light, and warmth, transforms us, bestowing on us something of his radiance. Those who are possessed by God resemble the burning log, which, St John of the Cross tells us, little by little becomes white-hot. Nourished by the fire of the Spirit, our life becomes fire. Is not this the fire of which Jesus spoke when he said; 'I have come to bring fire upon the earth . . .' (Lk 12 49).

N.P.

In prayer it is quality that counts: length of time is of secondary importance.

Malines 1974

It is one thing to speak *about* God, another to speak *to* God. And yet another to listen to God in deep silence.

N.P.

The Lord did not want his Apostles to live in a state of tension. He bade them; 'Come away into a quiet place'. 'Rest awhile,' he would say to them at the end of a demanding day.

C.L.D.D.

We need rest: rest in the ordinary sense of the word and rest in God. In the hurly-burly of our daily lives, we should make time for God.

ibid.

Thank you . . .

A thanksgiving can take the form of a litany in which I enumerate a name, a memory, a date, a coincidence. Or I say 'thank you' to God for advice in a moment of crisis, a book I have read, a telephone call, a letter, a suffering, a word of encouragement. And permeating these and binding them together is my gratitude for a joy and a peace which no man can take from me.

N.P.

'The Hound of Heaven' . . .

Each of us can interpret Francis Thompson's poem in the light of his own life. But the God who is 'on the watch', ready, like the 'heavenly hound', to pursue us with his love, is the same for all. His concern, multiplying itself to infinity, is there in its entirety for each one of us.

Malines 1974

Open the Gospel . . .

Open the Gospel and ask the Holy Spirit to shed his light – the love of God – upon the words confronting you. Jesus did not speak twenty centuries ago only. He is speaking, now, today.

New York 1972

Spontaneity . . .

Timidity, human respect, inhibitions, our education, condition us to assume a mask of reserve: we are ready to pray with our soul, not with our body. The young, who know nothing of our complexes, express themselves with much greater freedom.

N.P.

They appreciate spontaneity in prayer: rhythmic movement, clapping of hands; hands raised or joined as a sign of unity. Possibly the time has come to react somewhat against our misinterpretation of our Lord's invitation to worship in 'spirit and in truth'. After all, the Son of God became man and his religion embraces all that is human. A dehumanised spiritual life is contrary to the logic of the Incarnation: Jesus did not die to save souls – he died to save *men*.

Malines 1974

Afraid to believe . . .

We are afraid to believe who we are – we hesitate to have faith in the Christ who lives and acts within us. We have not the courage to believe in prayer which can include miracles.

Those concerned with the teaching of the Church should give new and deeper instruction on the meaning of prayer. We need to hear more about God's fatherly love; the God of the living, not of the dead; the source of good, not of evil, who wills always the well-being of his children.

N.P.

Our prayer must embrace the complexity of the world as it really is. There are sicknesses of many kind: visible, invisible, physical, psychological, pathological, those, too, which originate in some long forgotten traumatic experience. Our prayer should include all within us that is in need of healing: we must open ourselves in all the dimensions of our human suffering, past as well as present, to the light of God's grace. We should remember that Jesus is the same yesterday and today, that he is Lord of the past as well as the present.

ibid.

The prayer of adoration . . .

I love you, who have assembled here, because you praise God not for what he gives, but for his own sake, his glory. And this is more than natural, it is supernatural. If we ourselves were to compose the

Lord's prayer, we'd begin, I imagine: 'Give us TODAY, QUICKLY, our daily bread'. But you are asking for something greater: that the will of God, the glory of God, may become a reality. By the grace of the Holy Spirit you have discovered what adoration means.

I love you because you are faithful both to the Father and the Son; because you understand that Christians are not followers of Jesus as a Marxist is a follower of Marx or a Maoist a follower of Mao. You understand that the Jesus whom you follow is the Holy One, the Anointed.

Seventh International Conference on Catholic Charismatic Renewal. Notre Dame, Indiana 1973

Give us a heart for loving,
a heart of flesh and not of stone
for loving God and man.
Give us, we beg, your heart,
that we forget ourselves
in perfect love.

Christmas Prayer 1972

From a talk given on the radio at the time of a colliery disaster at Bois de Cazier, Marcinelle, Belgium ...

These afflicted men, women, and children should be enfolded in our prayers. Prayer alone can penetrate to the deepest level of the soul, like the rescue-worker who goes down the shaft. There are times when human speech has a hollow ring. There are wounds on which God alone can lay his hand. Only his grace can pierce the hard shell of sorrow, reveal a gleam of hope.

Who does not feel man's helplessness at such moments: the emptiness of conventional sympathy, words that have nothing to say about eternity, words without hope of a meeting hereafter, without hope of a resurrection? What can you say to a mother whose son's life has come to an end in the grave? What can you say to a wife whose husband is walled within the earth, as are those miners deep down in the pit – no hope of escape, no way into daylight?

Do not forget that you carry Christ within you, that his are the words of eternal life. Be another Christ. Bring words of life into these grieving homes. You must not speak as those who are without hope. You must not be content with conventional sympathy. Go to those who mourn. Show that Christ is speaking through you. If it be one word only, let it be charged with life and hope.

To those without faith suffering is a night in which no stars shine. For those who believe, light illumines the darkness.

ibid.

A time of waiting . . .

Reflect upon winter in the woods. Trees which seem to be devoid of life are waiting for the sap to rise. Lopped branches enable others to take their place. Winter is not death: it is preparation for life. Winter is not an end: it is a soil wherein the foliage of the future is nurtured Winter is not desolation: it is a time of waiting. It is darkness before the dawn.

ibid.

Extremes . . .

'Progressives' are in danger of losing the purity of doctrinal faith.

'Conservatives' show a lack of faith on the existential level: they lack faith in the active presence of the Holy Spirit in the Church today.

Le Soir 1969

In the words of an American theologian at the Council, I would say of my own position: 'I am at the extreme centre.'

ibid.

'You know neither the day nor the hour' (Matt 25 13)

We must learn to accept God's rhythm. He answers our prayers but in his own time. 'My thoughts' says the Lord, 'are not your thoughts, neither are your ways mine.' Leave all to him. Believe with resolute faith that 'all things work together for good, for those who love God.

C.L.D.D.

The Lord asks of us, as of his contemporaries, a faith that is expectant and confident, such as that of the woman, who, reaching out her hand and touching the hem of his garment, was healed by a power that went forth from him.

N.P.

Faith resembles an ancient oak tree. Its roots plunge into the nourishing soil of the Church's tradition. The sap, if it is to rise and give life to the tree, must be enclosed by a protective bark which forms gradually as the generations pass. The bark is not the sap, yet it derives its nourishment from the sap. The two are closely associated; whatever effects the outside of the tree effects the inside, too.

The life-giving sap within the tree of faith is the living word of God as he reveals himself. Our dogmas and theological formulae serve to protect and contain this sap. They derive nourishment from within. They are 'spirit and life'; but they are, to some extent, conditioned by their habitat and by the climate.

C.C.

Like the wise householder in the gospel, the Church takes from her treasure-house things new and old. Renewal of this kind may trouble those who want ready-made solutions, unchanging formulations, slick answers to problems. This cannot be helped.

C.C.

Faith is both certitude and searching.

It is right, therefore, that theologians should from time to time revise the formulae in which our dogmas and beliefs are worded.

C.C.

'Anyone who fails to love can never have known God, for God is love' (1 Jn 4 8). If a theologian is not to some extent a contemplative and a man striving for sanctity, his teaching inspires no confidence. This is stressed in the Eastern Churches. Evagrius says: 'If you truly pray, you are a theologian, and if you are a theologian you truly pray'. And St Macarius: 'A theologian is a man who has been taught by God'.

Let us pray, therefore, for the holiness of our theologians.

F.C.C.

To the eyes of faith ...

Christ did not come to explain suffering: he came to fill it with his presence, fill it to the brim, as we fill a cup; to make it live through his presence, make it – in the nature of a sacrament – a palpable instrument of grace. Suffering is participation in the mystery of Good Friday.

C.L.D.D.

On Good Friday darkness covered the earth and the disciples in anguish questioned one another. All seemed to have ended. And on the next day the women who came weeping, to embalm the body had on their lips one question only: 'Who will roll away for us the stone from the door of the tomb?'

In the sight of man it was midnight. But to the eyes of faith midnight heralds the dawn: the living Christ will rise, triumphant.

105

It is good in the darkness to believe in the light,
It is good amidst tears to believe in joy
It is good amidst death to believe in Life.

ibid.

Nothing is too small in the eyes of God. Everything has a meaning, a purpose, a significance. He knows all our deeds and actions; he follows and motivates them. This immense activity on the part of Providence weaves the web of life and binds the threads together.

ibid.

5. COURAGE, FIDELITY, HOPE, JOY

Courage

Do not be afraid. Cease to hug the shore. Make
for the open sea.

C.L.D.D.

A London newspaper advertised for volunteers
to go on an Antarctic expedition:

'Men wanted for a dangerous expedition. Low
pay. Intense cold, months of total darkness,
constant danger. Return uncertain. If
successful, honour and gratitude.'

There were five thousand replies from those who
wanted to go. Let us salute their courage. But it
was primarily physical courage. Moral courage is
more rare: the courage to do one's duty; go
against the current and the prevailing wind; face
irony and mockery. St Peter who trembled before
the ridicule of a maid-servant, attained something

of this. And it is this we must resolutely strive for: courage to face life; courage to accept life.

ibid.

You must have the courage to take literally some passages in the Gospels.

ibid.

As the time comes for the young to decide upon their future it is a splendid thing when parents have the courage not to stifle the generosity and idealism of their children, not to clip the wings of youth through a prudence that goes to excess.

Fathers and mothers, I beg you, give serious thought to this. Sometimes when the young get out of hand and want to follow mere caprice, you are justified in raising objections. But reflect; your opposition can be a revolt against the Holy Spirit at work within them and, therefore, an obstacle to God's grace. Your children are not your property. They belong to God: he entrusts them to you. In his name I plead their cause. Be on your guard against too much prudence, too much caution. Help them to make a good start.

ibid.

Courage can be acquired by prolonged training. A growing, continuous effort will banish from us fear of difficulties, rebuffs, objections. It will do away with the phantoms created by the imagination to deter us from taking decisive action. 'It is not the difficulty of something' Seneca says, 'that makes us afraid to venture, it is our *fear* that it will be difficult!'

G.E.C.

We need men with the courage to pay the price demanded by the Gospel.

We need the courage to remove from within the Church all that is not in accordance with the Gospel — all the dust that has accumulated down the centuries. We need the courage to walk on the waters, to face what is difficult, even impossible — we need to show that more often than one supposes, 'what is difficult can be done at once, what is impossible takes a bit longer'. Courage is nothing other than daily fidelity to the Holy Spirit within us, urging us to speak and to act when silence, compromise and passivity would be the comfortable, easy way . . . courage to be true to the Gospel, to believe that truth means liberty and justice.

Cambridge 1973

Pope John said 'Let's throw open the windows and let in the fresh air'.

Yes, yes, if you let in a draught you may catch cold, but if you keep the windows closed there is the greater danger of suffocation.

Malines 1973

May the Holy Spirit confer upon us, as he did upon the Apostles at Pentecost, the gift of 'courageous speech'. We are tempted to change St Paul's words, from Psalm 116, 'I believed and therefore I spoke,' into 'I believed and therefore kept silent'.

Cambridge 1973

Life is not worth living unless it is dedicated to values that transcend our everyday existence. Man is not created for life on 'ground-level'. His heart reaches beyond the confines of a house, however comfortable, however much a home it may be. The human heart must have its reasons for living: reasons which match its aspirations. The heart of man aspires to the infinite, the eternal: it dreams of surrendering to something above and beyond itself.

C.L.D.D.

Fidelity

The concept of fidelity implies faith in others. We are faithful not to ourselves, but to others or to God. Opponents of the indissolubility of the marriage bond use as arguments marriages hastily contracted, then broken up for some futile reason and given publicity in the press. These were probably unions undertaken merely on a legal basis, without genuine love or a mutual commitment for life. Hence it could be argued that there was no authentic marriage, that it was a question not of breaking the bond but of its non-existence.

The lived experience of christians who commit themselves in marriage, the priesthood, or the religious life, is quite different. This fidelity is not static. It has to be sufficiently flexible to adjust to changing circumstances, yet be resolute. Commitment of this kind means that I no longer allow myself to be torn asunder by fluctuations of instinct or emotion or by every whim. Through this commitment rooted in eternity and founded on the certitude of love for the Other or another, I polarise my life in a new way. Fidelity is not routine or fixity. It is a daily re-creation, enabling us to respond to varying circumstances; a victory over temptations, a way of making progress in the midst of trials: it alone renews youth.

This, the Gospel warns us, will demand renunciation: it will often demand that the 'grain of wheat die'. The dimension of eternity underlies the Lord's appeals on behalf of fidelity. 'What God has joined together let no man put asunder.'

Every commitment must be renewed, so that it may live and, moreover, nourish its resolution to be permanent. Speaking of fidelity between married couples, Maurice Zundel calls it 'an ever freer choice of an ever stronger love'.

There is pride in a continuity that is lived. Roger Garaudy writes: 'The joy of a man is to have remained faithful at sixty to the dream of his twenties'. Likewise, Alfred de Vigny: 'Life is a dream of youth realised in maturity'.

The commitment between husband and wife is magnificently expressed in the English marriage ritual:

I, N . . . take thee, N . . . to my wedded wife,
to have and to hold from this day forward,
for better for worse
for richer for poorer,
in sickness and in health,
to love and to cherish,
till death us do part,
according to God's holy ordinance;
and thereto I plight thee my troth.

Man's existence does not consist of solitary moments lived with intensity until they run out. On the contrary it is the continual decision to live each 'now' as the outcome of a 'before' and the preparation for an 'after'.

Fidelity, the fruit and condition of human commitment, certainly implies the will to live 'today' with intensity and totally; but what would be a 'total' gift if it excluded these two essential dimensions: the past and the future?

The concept of fidelity is valid for every human being, believer or non-believer. It derives however, singular support and strength from belief in God.

A Christian's fidelity is borne, sustained, and vivified by the fidelity of God himself. And this divine fidelity is at the heart of ours. It is, indeed, its most firm support. Through and in God husband and wife love each other not solely with a human love that is personal and fragile, but with God's own love. The sacrament of marriage penetrates the hearts of the man and the woman with its grace, thus raising them beyond themselves, making eternal in them and with them the love that brought them together.

When it is a question of fidelity as a priest or religious, God is yet more in the foreground. The words 'I know in whom I have believed' are the soul of every priestly and religious vocation.

Pastoralia 1972

We are familiar with Hans Christian

Andersen's story of the spider who, after spinning a beautiful web, tried to be free of the thread by which it hung from the branch. And so, thinking the thread superfluous, she cut it. The web immediately fell apart!

The same applies to society's dependence on God. Adherence to God brings coherence among men: the vertical link between God and man is essential to the horizontal link between man and man.

From the Address given by Cardinal Suenens
on the occasion of the award of the
Templeton Prize.

The world is destroying itself through atheism and lack of faith. This is the tragedy of our times. It is not true that man, as is sometimes said, is not capable of managing the world without God. The truth is that without God he can only, in the last analysis, build a world that is hostile and dangerous to man. That is how things stand at the present moment. As a consequence of no longer recognising God, it becomes more and more necessary to defend man against man. Severed from God, man does not recognise his neighbour: *homo homini lupus*.

ibid.

Hope

A true christian is a man of hope. A disciple of Christ, St Peter tells us, when asked the ground for the hope that is his, should have his answer ready. Hope is a component factor of our very being. In some quarters today hope has a bad press.

N.P.

We must take hold of hope and restore it to its rightful place; for hope, as always, is a theological virtue, a dynamic reality within us which derives from God and relies on God: God alone. Hope makes mockery of our ponderous statistics, probability charts, prognostications: it goes its own way despite our forecasts. 'My thoughts are not your thoughts, neither are your ways my ways, says the Lord.' Hope is the servant of God: 'the master of the impossible.'

ibid.

To hope is a duty, not a luxury.

ibid.

To hope is not to dream, but to turn dreams into a reality.

ibid.

115

The Church lives by a hope that is centred in God. She offers us a hope which 'surpasses all that the eyes of man have seen, all his ears have heard: a hope which is none other than that which God has prepared for those whom he loves'.

E.F.T.

The Lord we need is a living God: a sign of hope, a star in the darkness. We are discovering afresh not only Jesus as Lord, but the Spirit of Jesus in our midst. The emphasis on the Holy Spirit in our times is indeed a sign of hope. But we need a renewed encounter with, a new surrender to, the Holy Spirit. In charismatic renewal this encounter, this surrender has begun to take shape.

Milwaukee. U.S.A. 1973

The christian of tomorrow will not be able to face the future if we have not passed on to him a Christianity full of hope.

N.P.

Pope John said: 'I've never seen a pessimist

who has contributed anything useful to the world'.

Vatican II Anniversary Nov. 1970

Three favourite quotations from Pope John

'This year's celebration for my priestly jubilee have come to an end. What embarrassment it has caused me! Numerous priests dead or still alive after twenty five years in the priesthood have done wonders in the apostolate and in the sanctification of souls. And I, what have I done? Jesus, have mercy on me! But while I abase myself for the little or nothing I have done up to now, I lift up my eyes to the future. There is still light ahead of me; still hope of doing some good. And so I take up my staff again – even if it be the staff of an ageing man, and I go forward to meet whatever the Lord asks of me.'

Sofia October 30 1929

'I rejoice when I recall all the graces I have received from the Lord, but am ashamed for having been so niggardly in the use of my talents; my return is out of all proportion to the gifts I have received. Here is a mystery which makes me shudder, yet at the same time goads me on to action.'

August 10, 1961

117

'The Vicar of Christ! I don't deserve this title at all. I, the poor son of Baptist and Mary Ann Roncalli, both good christians, to be sure, but so unobtrusive, so humble.'

August 15, 1961

A few weeks before he died Pope John said: 'Every day is a good day to be born, every day a good day to die. "I know him in whom I have believed." ' He met his end with the serenity of a child going home, knowing his father would be there with open arms.

When he heard some of his household mourning at his bedside he protested: 'Don't weep, this is a time of joy'. As the end drew near he asked to be 'left alone with the Lord', to recollect himself. He could be heard repeating the Lord's words: 'I am the Resurrection and the Life. . . .' Then to the Blessed Virgin: 'My mother, my hope'. That was the end.

Homily in Commemoration of
Pope John delivered on October 28th 1963.

To confess the faith in the world of today requires that we have joy. Too many christians lack joy. The greatest reproach addressed to a christian is contained in the question: 'Why are you sad? For what are you waiting? If you are waiting for Christ, if each day is bringing you nearer to him, if you are convinced that he is deep within you, transforming your life into light, why are you sad?' John Henry Newman when speaking of having something to give to everyone, said that he could give hope in all circumstances, even in the face of death. We must not live as though we had no hope (1 Thess 4 13). We must not only construct a theology of hope, we must be the presence of hope.

Oxford 1973

Joy

It is a christian's role to reveal to his fellow-men that joy is a flower which can only open and bloom in the nourishing soil of hope, which is born of God and finds fulfilment in him.

Jesus opened the Sermon on the Mount with a cascade of words – the same word again and again: *Blessed* are the poor in spirit, *blessed* are the gentle, *blessed* are the peace-makers, *blessed* at those who mourn.

The words 'blessed' and 'happy' are at the very essence of the christian life. That is not to say life

119

is without suffering, without set-backs. No, joy and suffering exist side by side. But they are not on the same level, for suffering cannot vitiate hope. Joy is at a depth beyond the reach of man. Christ made a solemn promise to his followers: 'I shall give you a joy which no man can take from you'. Yes, it was a solemn promise, a sacred pledge.

C.L.D.D.

Man lives by joy more than he lives by bread.
ibid.

All the Church's joy is Easter joy.
ibid.

Let the bells ring out for joy the *alleluia* of the risen Christ.
ibid.

I ask you to open your heart to God's welcome, to his fatherly love for each of us. I ask you to say to him: 'Father, I trust in your love for me'. May this trust open your heart to joy! A joy which the world can neither give, nor take away.
ibid.

We must not live in a dream-world. We must not fall back on alibis nor wait for tomorrow or the next day to do something 'grand' with our life. Now is the acceptable time, now the moment that the Master has ordained. He waits for us: 'Behold, I stand at the door and knock'. That is what the Lord says to each one of us.

ibid.

BIBLIOGRAPHY

Books written by Cardinal Suenens that have appeared in English.

Theology of the Apostolate, Mercier Press, Cork, 1953

Edel Quinn, Fallon Ltd, Dublin, 1953

The Right View of Moral Re-armament, Burns and Oates, London, 1953

The Gospel to Every Creature, Burns and Oates, London, 1956

Mary the Mother of God, Hawthorn Books, New York, 1957

Love and Control, Burns and Oates, London, 1961

The Nun in the World, Burns and Oates, London, 1962

Christian Life Day by Day, Burns and Oates, London, 1963

The Church in Dialogue, Fides Publishers, Notre Dame, Indiana, 1965

Co-Responsibility in the Church, Burns and Oates, London/Herder and Herder New York, 1968

The Future of the Christian Church, (Michael Ramsey and L–J Suenens) SCM Press, London/Morehouse–Barlow, New York, 1970

A New Pentecost?, Darton, Longman and Todd, London/Seabury Press, New York, 1975

A biography of Cardinal Suenens has also been published in English:

Cardinal Suenens, A Portrait by Elizabeth Hamilton, Hodder and Stoughton, London/ Doubleday, New York, 1975